REALITY STAR
The Way to Bla...
Luke Edwards

I0697579

What is a Reality Star?

A reality star is a person who has become known through their participation in reality shows or through their presence on social media. These types of stars can come from different areas, such as the entertainment industry, the fashion industry, sports or even everyday life. The term "reality TV" was introduced in the 1990s to describe shows that depict people's lives in a documentary-like manner. Some of the most popular reality shows include formats such as "Big Brother," "Survivor," "The Bachelor," and "Keeping Up with the Kardashians." These shows often have a reputation for producing drama, conflict, and controversial content to grab viewers' attention. Reality stars often have a large number of fans gained through their appearances on the shows or their online presence. Many of them use their fame to advance their careers by appearing in films, television series or music videos or by starting their own brand. However, there are also critics who view reality stars as superficial and unimportant. Some argue that these stars have no special skills or talents and that their fame is based solely on their ability to stand in front of the camera and attract media attention. Another problem that comes with reality star fame is the possibility of cyberbullying and harassment. Due to their constant presence on social media and in the public eye, reality stars often become the target of online trolls and unpleasant comments. However, reality stars can also have positive effects. Many of them use their platform to address important issues and draw attention to social problems. Some reality stars have also founded charitable organizations and are involved in charitable causes. Overall, a reality star is a person who has become known due to their presence in the public and media. Although they may be viewed by some as superficial and insignificant, they can also have a positive impact by addressing important issues and supporting charitable causes.

Why do you want to be a reality star?

The motivation to become a reality star can be different for different people. Some possible reasons for this could be the following. 1. Fame: A major incentive for many people to become reality stars is the desire for fame and notoriety. By participating in reality shows, they can present themselves to a wide audience and increase their popularity. This type of celebrity can open up new career opportunities for them, such as becoming an influencer, actor, or TV host. 2. Money: Another important factor in deciding to become a reality star is the potential earning potential. Reality stars can earn money through endorsement deals, sponsorships, public appearances and other activities. Some reality stars have managed to amass considerable wealth through their appearances. 3. Adventure: For some people, the appeal of becoming a reality star is the adventure and the opportunity to have new experiences. Participating in reality shows can give them the opportunity to take part in exciting activities and challenges that they would never have experienced otherwise. 4. Self-realization: Some reality stars have a desire to self-actualize and showcase their personality and talents to a wide audience. By participating in reality shows, they can increase their self-confidence and self-esteem and explore their skills and passions. 5. Career: Reality stars can also benefit from wanting to break into the entertainment industry. Participating in reality shows can give them the opportunity to make connections that can be beneficial to their future careers. Some reality stars have managed to break into the industry and build careers in the music, film or television industries. 6. Easy access to celebrity: Reality shows offer many people easy access to celebrity. By participating in these shows, they can become famous in a short period of time and gain a large number of fans. This allows them to attract the attention of companies and celebrities and accelerate their careers. 7. The chance to make a difference: Some reality stars also want to take the opportunity to spread a message or advocate for a cause they care about. Participating in reality shows can give them the opportunity to present their concerns and ideas to a wide audience and raise awareness about certain issues. 8. The chance to win something: Another incentive for participating in reality shows can be the chance to win something. Many reality shows offer prizes and rewards for participants, such as cash prizes, trips, or vouchers. Overall, there are many reasons why someone would want to become a reality star.

Prepare for your life as a reality star

Being a reality star can be an exciting and lucrative adventure, but it also requires a lot of work and preparation. Here are some steps you can take to prepare for life as a reality star. 1. Develop your personality: Reality stars often have a strong and memorable personality that sets them apart from others. Start developing your own personality by focusing on your strengths and interests. Think about what makes you unique and interesting and how you can emphasize those characteristics to appeal to the audience. 2. Hone your skills: Reality stars often have a specific skill or talent that they can showcase on the show. Whether it's singing, dancing, cooking, or another skill, practice and hone your skills so you can showcase them on the show. 3. Be willing to share your personal life: One of the most difficult challenges as a reality star is sharing your personal life. You have to be ready to share your thoughts and feelings with the world and open yourself up to the cameras. Think about which parts of your life you want to share and which you don't. 4. Build your network: Reality stars are often known for their connections and network of contacts. Start building your own network by building relationships with other people in the industry. Go to events and events where you can meet potential connections, and use social media platforms like Instagram and Twitter to network. 5. Learn to market yourself: As a reality star, you must learn to market yourself and maintain your image. Think about how you want to present yourself on social media platforms and what type of image you want to build. Make sure you present your brand and image consistently to appeal to a larger audience.6. Be ready for fame: If you are successful as a reality star, you will quickly become famous. Be ready for media and audience attention and interest. Think about how you will deal with fans approaching you or paparazzi following you. Also think about how you will protect your privacy and deal with criticism. 7. Find an agency or manager: An agency or manager can help you advance your career as a reality star and give you access to more opportunities. Look for an agency or manager who has experience in the industry and can help you promote your image and brand. 8. Educate yourself: As a reality star, you must constantly learn and grow to stay competitive. Educate yourself by attending courses or workshops.

Choose the right reality TV show

Reality TV shows have gained enormous popularity in recent years. From music competitions to dating shows to survival formats, there are a variety of options to choose from. However, choosing the right reality TV show can be difficult. Here are some things to consider to make the best choice. Choosing the right reality TV show depends on your own interests and preferences. For example, if you enjoy listening to music and singing, you might be interested in a singing competition show like "The Voice" or "American Idol." If you love sports, you could choose a show like "American Ninja Warrior" or "Survivor." If you have a romantic streak, you could be interested in a dating show like "The Bachelor" or "Love Island". It's important to consider your own interests and preferences to get the best possible experience. Choosing a show that doesn't match your interests can quickly become boring and uninteresting. It is always a good idea to check the ratings and reviews of a reality TV show before watching it. There are many online platforms like IMDb or Rotten Tomatoes where you can read reviews from other viewers and get an idea of how good the show is. Additionally, you can also ask friends and family who may have already seen the show to hear their opinions and experiences. Ratings and reviews can help one manage expectations and decide whether the show is worth a try. Reality TV shows come in different formats and lengths. Some shows have a fixed number of episodes while others air weekly. It's important to consider the format and length of the show to ensure you have enough time to see it. If you're short on time, it might be best to choose a show with fewer episodes or a shorter runtime. However, if you have a lot of time, you could opt for a show that airs weekly and lasts for several month. Consider the credibility and authenticity of the show It. is also important to consider the credibility and authenticity of the reality TV show. Some shows are known for staging or manipulating scenes to create more drama and tension. If you prefer a show with a more authentic approach, you could opt for a documentary reality show like "The Amazing Race" or "Queer Eye." It's also important to note that reality TV shows are often part of a larger marketing strategy and that the personalities featured on the show may not be exactly as they portray themselves.

Apply for the reality TV show

If you are interested in applying for a reality TV show, there are a few steps you need to follow to make your application successful. Here are some tips on how to go about it. Choose a show First, you need to decide which reality TV show you want to apply for. There are many different shows, all with different requirements and audiences. So think carefully about which show suits you and your abilities best. Once you find a show that interests you, you need to read the requirements. In most cases, there is a list of criteria you must meet in order to apply. This may include things like age, location, experience in certain areas or personality traits. Make sure you meet all requirements before submitting your application. Typically, to apply for a reality TV show, you will need to create a video. In this video you should introduce yourself and explain why you are the perfect candidate for the show. It's also a good idea to show off your personality and skills, perhaps by showcasing some of your hobbies or skills. In addition to the video, you should also write a letter introducing yourself and explaining your reasons for wanting to participate in the show. You should also emphasize why you think you will do well on the show. You should also include some photos of yourself to showcase your personality and appearance. These photos should be current and should represent you well. Once you have completed your application, you must send it to the production company or broadcaster that is producing the show. Make sure you submit all required documents including the application form, videos, briefs and photos. Be patient You will usually receive a response to your application within a few weeks.

However, in some cases it may take longer. Be patient and wait for a response. If you get a rejection, don't be discouraged and try another show. Stay positive Stay positive and open-minded during the application process. You should remember that reality TV shows are very competitive and you may have many competitors. Make sure you put your best foot forward and do your best to catch the producers' attention.

Prepare for the casting

Reality shows are very popular these days and offer many people the chance to showcase themselves on television. An important part of this process is casting. Here are some tips on how to prepare for a reality show casting. Find out about the show First, you should find out about the reality show you want to apply for. Watch a few episodes and familiarize yourself with the concept and rules. Understanding what's important in the show will help you decide how you want to present yourself. Identify your strengths When you apply, you should focus on your strengths and talents. Think about what you are particularly good at and what characteristics make you stand out. For example, if you have a great personality or are talented in a particular area, you should highlight that in your application. Practice your skills If you are applying for a reality show that requires specific skills, you should practice and improve them. For example, if there is a cooking show, you should cook several dishes and improve your skills. If it is a dance show, you should practice your dancing skills. Practicing will help you appear more confident and prepared. Plan Your Outfits Your looks are important when it comes to applying for a reality show. Plan your outfits carefully and make sure you look and feel your best. Choose clothes that fit your style and personality and that put you in a good light. Familiarize yourself with the casting process Every reality show has its own casting process. Educate yourself about the process so you know what to expect. You may need to make a video of yourself or you may be invited for an interview. Make sure you are aware of all requirements and deadlines and meet them. When applying for a reality show, it's important to be authentic. Don't try to be someone else or play a role. Just be yourself and show your personality. Producers are looking for unique and interesting personalities, so be honest and authentic. If you are invited to a casting, you should be well prepared. Bring all required documents and make sure you are on time. Also prepare for possible questions and consider how best to answer them. Casting for a reality show is all about putting yourself out there and showing that you have what it takes to make it on television. Be yourself.

Negotiate your contract

Negotiating a reality show contract requires careful consideration and planning to ensure that the interests of all parties are taken into account. This article discusses the steps and strategies that can be helpful when negotiating a reality show contract. Before you start negotiating, you need to know your goals and priorities. What are your most important concerns? Would you like to earn a certain amount as a fee? Or maybe you want to promote your own brand and reach a larger audience? The better you understand your goals and priorities, the better you will be able to negotiate and achieve the best results. You also need to understand what you can offer the show and the network. You should understand your strengths and your niche. For example, if you are an expert in a certain field, you can use that as a selling point. If you have a large social media following, you can also use that as an argument. The better you understand what you are worth, the better you can strengthen your position in negotiations. It is important to know your negotiating partners in order to better communicate with them and understand their interests. Who are the producers of the show? Who are the network managers? What is her background and story? The better you understand your negotiating partners, the better you can understand their needs and concerns and therefore negotiate better. Write down all the conditions you want to discuss. What is your fee? How long is the show? What rights do you have to your image and your name? What happens if you get injured or your career is affected because of the show? Having all the terms and conditions in writing can help ensure nothing is missed. Negotiate every point of the contract. Don't be shy when it comes to your salary, your role in the show and your requirements. If you have an idea of what you want and what you are worth, you should share this with your negotiating partners and ask them for the best. You can also negotiate other incentives such as a larger social media presence, more advertising time, or other perks. 6. Keep Your Emotions in Control It's important to remain calm and professional when negotiating. Negotiations can get emotional, but controlling your emotions will help you better represent your interests. If you feel like negotiations are stalled or could lead to an argument, take a break and think about your next steps. Get help It's a good idea to get professional help when implementing a contract.

Become part of the reality TV team

If you dream of becoming part of a reality TV team, there are some steps you can take to increase your chances. Here are some tips that can help you. Choose the right reality TV format. There are many different types of reality TV shows, from competitions like "American Idol" and 'Survivor" to shows that document the daily lives of celebrities or everyday people . Choose the format that best suits your interests and skills. For example, if you are a passionate singer, it makes sense to apply for a show like "The Voice". Make a Compelling Application Most reality TV shows require you to fill out an application or submit a video introducing yourself and explaining why you are suitable for the show. It is important to create a compelling application that highlights your personality, skills and experience and shows why you are suitable for the show's format. Make sure your application is neat and well structured and that you provide all required information. Build a Strong Online Presence. In today's world, reality TV producers often look for contestants with a strong online presence. Create a website or blog that showcases your personality, interests, and experiences. Also use social media like Instagram, Twitter and TikTok to show your personality and life. Make sure you design your presence in a way that suits your target audience and reflects their interests. Be Open to Experiences. The world of reality TV is often about having new experiences and taking on challenges. Be open to new experiences and show that you are willing to step out of your comfort zone. For example, if you have never danced before but are applying for a dance show, you should show that you are willing to work hard and learn new skills. It can be helpful to network with other reality TV contestants to share experiences and possibly even get recommendations. Search for online communities or attend events where former reality TV contestants appear or speak. This can help you make contacts and increase your chances of a successful application. Prepare for the casting.If you are invited for a casting, it is important to prepare well. Familiarize yourself with the format of the show and consider how best to present yourself. Also think about what questions you might be asked and prepare answers accordingly.

Create a personality for yourself

A reality show can be a great opportunity to showcase your personality and share your life in front of a wide audience. If you are interested in creating a personality for yourself on a reality show, there are some steps you can take to make it happen. Before going on a reality show, it is important that you know your strengths and weaknesses. By identifying your strengths and talents, you can focus on situations where you can shine and stand out from other participants. Likewise, it is important to know your weaknesses so that you can prepare to overcome them on the show and improve yourself. One of the most important requirements for success on a reality show is having a unique personality that stands out from other contestants. Think about what makes you unique and what qualities or skills you have that others don't have. Try to emphasize these qualities in the show to leave a lasting impression on viewers. While it is important to have a unique personality, it is equally important to remain authentic. Don't try to be someone you're not to please on the show. Viewers will notice if you're not being authentic, and it can affect your credibility. On a reality show, conflict is often staged to heighten the drama. It is important that you learn how to deal with conflict and how to communicate your opinions effectively without being aggressive. This will help ensure that you are respected and that your personality is perceived positively. One of the most important skills in a reality show is the ability to communicate effectively. Learn to speak clearly and express your thoughts and feelings. Good communication skills will help you have a positive impact on viewers and strengthen your personality. A reality show often requires you to take risks and get out of your comfort zone. Be willing to try new things and push your limits. This will help you develop your personality and show viewers that you are bold and confident. 7. Stay positive and solution-oriented A positive attitude and the ability to find solutions to problems are important qualities in a reality show.

Build your own brand

A reality show can be a great platform to build a brand. Here are some steps you can take to build a successful brand on a reality show. Identify a niche that is unique to you and that you believe will provide a strong foundation for your brand. For example, if you're appearing on a cooking show, you might focus on a specific dish or style of cooking that is unique to you. This will help you stand out from the other participants and establish your brand. A reality show is all about showing personality. Make sure you stay true to yourself and let your personality shine through in every episode. Show your strengths, but also your weaknesses. When you are authentic, you will build stronger trust with viewers and be able to successfully establish your brand. Social media can be a great way to build your brand and increase your reach. Use social media platforms like Instagram, Facebook, Twitter or TikTok to reach and engage with your audience. Post content regularly to maintain interest in your brand. It is important that your brand is consistent and consistent across all channels. This includes your name, logo, colors and font. Make sure your brand is clear and consistent so your viewers can easily recognize and remember it. In a reality show, you usually collaborate with other contestants. Use this opportunity to promote your brand. Connect with other participants and work together to achieve common goals. If you build a good relationship with the other participants, you can support each other and build your brand together. Take advantage of every opportunity to promote your brand. This includes interviews, photo shoots and promotions. For example, if you are interviewed in a magazine, use this opportunity to showcase your brand. Share the interview on social media platforms to increase your reach. It is important that you stay active and continue to promote your brand even after the show ends. Use social media to keep your fans updated and share in your journey. Stay active to keep your brand alive

Use social media

Social media plays an important role in today's world and influences almost all aspects of our lives. Reality shows are no exception as they appeal to a wide range of viewers and provide a platform to connect with them. In this article, I will discuss how social media can be used on a reality show and how it affects viewers. Hashtags are an important part of social media and can help content go viral on platforms like Twitter, Instagram, and TikTok. Reality shows often use this feature by creating hashtags that include the name of the show or the name of the characters. These hashtags are then displayed on screens during the broadcast or on social media platforms to encourage viewers to use them. When viewers use the hashtags, they can share their posts with other fans of the show and share their thoughts and opinions with them. One of the most important features of social media is the ability to engage directly with fans. Reality shows can take advantage of this by creating social media profiles for their characters or hosting live chats with the cast. Through this interaction, fans can ask questions, get to know their favorite characters, and connect with other fans of the show. This increases viewer engagement and can help them feel more connected to the show. Reality shows can post teasers and trailers on social media platforms to get viewers excited about upcoming episodes or seasons. These teasers may include short clips from upcoming episodes or interviews with the characters. By sharing these teasers on social media platforms, reality shows can build viewer anticipation and capture the attention of those who may not have heard of the show. Another advantage of social media is the ability to conduct polls and surveys. Reality shows can use this feature to learn viewers' opinions and preferences. For example, they can conduct polls about their favorite characters or what's happening in the current episode. These polls can also help viewers learn more about the characters and relate to them better. Fan Clubs Social media is also a great place for fans to organize and form fan clubs. Reality shows can use these fan clubs to keep viewers engaged with the show and increase their loyalty. These fan clubs can be set up on social media platforms such as Facebook or Instagram and can include discussion forums, competitions and other activities to keep viewers entertained

Use your fans

As a reality star, your fans are an important part of your success. They are your supporters, your followers and your brand ambassadors. But how do you best use your fans to advance your career and expand your reach? In this article, we will give you some tips on how to make the most of your fans as a reality star. It is important to stay in touch with your fans to build a relationship and retain them. Use social media platforms like Instagram, Twitter and Facebook to regularly interact with your fans and keep them updated about your current projects. You can also live stream on Instagram or Facebook to directly address your fans and answer questions. Offer your fans exclusive content that they can't find anywhere else. This can be, for example, behind-the-scenes material from filming or personal insights into your life as a reality star. This creates a connection between you and your fans and increases the likelihood that they will support your brand and share your content. Meet-and-greets are a great way to get to know your fans in person and reinforce your brand. For example, you can organize a meet-up after an event or run an exclusive meet-and-greet competition on social media platforms. It is important to value your fans and give them the opportunity to get close to you and have an experience with you as a reality star. A fan club is a great way to organize and engage your fans. For example, you can create an exclusive Facebook group in which your fans can be informed about current projects and news. A fan club also allows you to reward your fans and offer them exclusive content or merchandise offers. Merchandise is a great way to strengthen your brand and generate additional income. Sell t-shirts, hats, or other items related to your reality star image. You can promote your merchandise offerings through your social media platforms or sell through an online store. Give your fans a glimpse into your career as a reality star. For example, you can write a blog or produce YouTube videos in which you share your experiences and tips. This builds trust and credibility with your fans and gives them insight into the world of reality TV. Use influencer marketing to expand your reach and spread the word about your brand. Use your relationships with other reality stars or influencers to create joint projects or campaigns

Use the scandal

As a reality star, there are many ways you can use a scandal to boost your career and notoriety. Of course, it is important to emphasize that not all scandals have positive effects and some can have negative consequences. So it's important to keep in mind that it's important to proceed responsibly and carefully. As a reality star, you have access to a wide audience through various social media platforms such as Instagram, TikTok, Twitter, and YouTube. Use these channels to explain your point of view or to describe the situation from your perspective. This can help your fans and followers come to your page and understand your perspective. It's important to stay calm and professional, even if you're caught up in a scandal. Avoid posting things on social media that are impulsive or emotional. Make sure your reactions to the situation are appropriate and try to keep a positive attitude. A scandal can also be an opportunity to learn and grow from your mistakes. If you made a mistake, be honest and admit that you were wrong. Try to make a positive change and involve your fans and followers in the process. A scandal can also help you gain media attention. Use this opportunity to give interviews or take part in discussions organized by various media outlets. This can help increase your exposure and advance your career. One way to get out of a scandal is to connect with your fans. Explain your perspective and connect with your fans on a more personal level. It's important to be transparent and honest to regain the trust of your fans. A scandal can leave you feeling overwhelmed and your career in jeopardy. It's important to not let it get you down and continue to work hard to advance your career. Stay positive and focused on your goals and try to make the best of every situation. Use the scandal as an opportunity. A scandal can also be an opportunity to develop yourself further as a reality star. If you have a new perspective on life or want to achieve new goals, use this opportunity to reposition yourself and take your career to the next level. Finally, it is important to emphasize that a scandal is not always positive and that it is important to act responsibly and forwardly

Create a fan base

As a reality star, it is important to build a loyal fan base to promote your career and increase your exposure. Here are some tips on how to build a fan base and maximize your public exposure. Fans are attracted to personalities that are authentic and honest. Stay true to yourself and show your personality in a natural way. Don't try to be someone you're not to get fans' attention. Social media platforms like Instagram, Twitter, TikTok and YouTube are great tools to interact with fans and increase your public presence. Make sure you regularly post content that showcases your personality and life. Use relevant hashtags to optimize your posts and increase visibility. Host meet-and-greets or autograph sessions to meet fans and build personal connections. These types of events can also help strengthen your brand and expand your fan base. Collaboration with other influencers can increase your reach. Look for influencers who align with your brand and suggest collaborations that can benefit both parties. Attend events related to your brand, such as television appearances, trade shows or charity events. These events can help increase your public exposure and attract new fans. As a reality star, it is important to have a unique personality and style to stand out from others. Find out what makes you unique and emphasize these qualities in your appearance. Maintain positive relationships with your fans by responding to comments, answering personal messages, and being grateful for their support. This type of engagement can help strengthen your fans' loyalty and expand your fan base. Participate in charitable activities to have a positive impact on your community and fan base. Donate to nonprofit organizations or participate in fundraising events. Building a fan base takes time, patience and persistence. It's important to regularly post content, interact with fans, and attend public events to maximize your public exposure.

Find sponsors

As a reality star, you probably have a certain level of notoriety and a loyal fan base. There are many ways to find sponsors who might be interested in working with you. Here are some tips that can help you find sponsors: Identify your niche audience and target group. You should know who your fans are and what their interests are. For example, if you appear on a cooking reality show, it would make sense to focus on food and kitchen equipment sponsors that might be interested in working with you. If you're appearing on a music reality show, it might make sense to focus on sponsors who are interested in the music industry. Create a professional website or social media presence. A professional website or social media presence can show potential sponsors that you are seriously interested in working with them and that you have a loyal following. Such exposure can also help improve your image and brand. Connecting with other reality stars and influencers can help you expand your reach and strengthen your brand. If you work with other celebrities, sponsors may also be interested in working with you to promote their products and services to a larger audience. There are many potential sponsors who might be interested in working with reality stars. Examples include brands that specialize in fashion, beauty, health and fitness, as well as companies that operate in the entertainment industry. You should identify the brands and companies that fit your target audience and reach out to them. When engaging with potential sponsors, you should create a compelling presentation showcasing your exposure, reach, and audience. You should also explain why you are interested in working with each sponsor and how you can help promote their products and services. Sponsors usually want to see something in return for their investment in you. So you should offer attractive services, such as social media posts, live events or product placement in your reality shows. These services should help strengthen the sponsor's image and brand and help them attract new customers. When entering into negotiations with a potential sponsor, you should negotiate carefully to ensure you reach a fair agreement

Market yourself

As a reality star, you have the opportunity to market yourself and your image to gain more exposure and career opportunities. Here are some tips on how to successfully market yourself as a reality star. As a reality star, you should make sure that you have an active and present role on social media. You should present yourself on platforms like Instagram, TikTok, Twitter, and YouTube to build your fan base and increase your exposure. Regularly post photos, videos and stories from your everyday life, your career and your projects to inspire your fans and let them participate in your life. Use your fame as a reality star to appear in other reality shows or talk shows. This will increase your presence on television and get additional attention from your fans. You also have the chance to gain new fans and expand your reach. As a reality star, you have the opportunity to sell merchandise and your own products. For example, you can have T-shirts, posters or other accessories printed with your name or picture and sell them online. Your fans can also purchase their own products such as beauty products or sportswear. By selling your own products, you not only earn additional income, but also increase your visibility. As a reality star, you often have the opportunity to collaborate with brands. Brands often look for well-known personalities to promote their products or to use them as ambassadors. By collaborating with brands, you can earn additional income and gain further attention from your fans. As a reality star, you have the chance to further advance your career in the entertainment industry. For example, you can work as a presenter, appear as an actress in films or series, or start a career in the music industry as a singer. Because of your fame, you often have an advantage when looking for new career opportunities. Charity work and social commitment. As a reality star, you have the opportunity to get involved in charitable causes and social projects. Because of your popularity, you often have a large reach and can therefore get more people interested in your projects. You can also strengthen your image as a role model and committed personality through your charity work and your social commitment. Overall, there are many ways to successfully market yourself as a reality star. It is important that you remain authentic and plan your image and career carefully.

Transform yourself into a brand

As a reality star, it can be difficult to stand out from the crowd and establish a strong public presence. One way to achieve this is by building a personal brand that showcases your unique personality traits and skills. Here are some steps you can take to transform yourself into a strong brand as a reality star. Before you start building your brand, it is important to have a clear concept that describes who you are and what sets you apart. Here you should think about your personality, interests, values and goals and how you can integrate these into your brand. The goal is to create a consistent image of yourself that attracts and engages your fans and followers. As a reality star, social media is a powerful tool to build your brand. Create accounts on all relevant platforms such as Instagram, TikTok, Twitter and Facebook and regularly share posts that reflect your brand and personality. Use hashtags and keywords that support your brand to make your posts more visible. An important aspect of building a strong brand as a reality star is sharing your story and experiences. Share your experiences on the reality show and give your fans a glimpse into your personality and life. Use your social media accounts to show behind the scenes of your life and career and show what makes you unique. One way to strengthen your brand is to collaborate with other brands that suit you. Consider partners who share your interests and values and with whom you can build a long-term relationship. This collaboration can help expand your brand and provide your fans and followers with a wider range of content. Another way to build your brand as a reality star is by selling products that reflect your personality. Consider developing merchandise products that your fans can purchase to show their support for your brand. These products can range from clothing and accessories to books and music, depending on your interests and abilities. 6. Get involved with charities: Another important aspect of building a strong brand as a reality star is getting involved with charities and non-profit organizations. Choose organizations that match your interests and values and become actively involved in their activities and projects.

Face the criticism

As a reality star you are often in the spotlight and there are many people who have an opinion about you. Sometimes these opinions can be expressed in the form of criticism. It is important to learn how to accept and deal with constructive criticism in order to grow and improve as a person. Here are some tips on how to face criticism as a reality star: Understand that criticism is normal. As a reality star, you are in the public eye and therefore subject to criticism. It is important to understand that criticism is a normal part of life and that everyone will be criticized at some point. Try not to be taken personally and remember that criticism can help you improve. When you are criticized, take time to listen and understand what the person is saying. Try not to react defensively or justify yourself. Instead, ask questions and try to see the situation from the perspective of the person criticizing you. There is a difference between constructive criticism and negative criticism. Constructive criticism is helpful and gives you ideas on how you can improve. Negative criticism, on the other hand, is often useless and only serves to hurt you or make you feel bad. Try to accept constructive criticism and ignore negative criticism. When you receive constructive criticism, use this opportunity to grow and improve. Try to implement the suggestions and improve yourself. However, if you feel like the criticism is unwarranted or misplaced, then let it go and focus on what you do well. It may be difficult, but try to be grateful for the criticism. Criticism can help uncover mistakes you might not have noticed otherwise. It can also help you improve and become more successful. As a reality star, receiving criticism can be lonely. Seek support from friends, family or a coach. They can help you process the criticism and give you ideas on how to improve. Overall, as a reality star, it's important to learn how to accept and deal with criticism. Criticism can help you improve and become more successful if you use it correctly. Try to accept constructive criticism and ignore negative criticism. Learn from the criticism and be grateful for it. Seek support when you need it.

Be ready for competition

The entertainment industry has changed a lot in recent years. Reality shows have become a staple of television programming and have created a new generation of stars. For many people, the dream of being on a reality show has become a reality. If you are also interested in a career as a reality star, you should be ready to face the competition. In this article, we will share some tips on how to prepare for a career as a reality star. Authenticity is one of the most important factors for success on a reality show. If you're not real, viewers will quickly see through you. Don't try to be someone you're not, just stay true to yourself. You should also be open and share your feelings and thoughts. Viewers want to see someone they can relate to, so let your personality shine through. Reality shows are usually very stressful and can involve unpredictable situations. You should therefore prepare well and be able to react quickly to changes. Make sure you familiarize yourself with the rules and procedures of the show and prepare for possible challenges. You should also be physically and emotionally ready as filming is often very long and tiring. On a reality show, you will likely have to work with other contestants. It is important that you are a team player and can work well with other people. Be prepared to compromise and support your colleagues. Not only will this lead to a better working atmosphere, but it will also help you be better received by viewers. Although reality shows often seem very casual and informal, it is important to remain professional. Be respectful of other participants, crew and producers. Make sure you are on time and follow the rules. Remember that on a reality show you are showcasing your skills and personality, so do your best. The competition in the world of reality shows is fierce. To be successful, you must stand out from the other participants. Make sure you have something unique to offer, be it your personality, your skills, or your story. Be creative and use your strengths to stand out from the rest. A career as a reality star requires hard work and dedication. It may take a long time to become successful, so stay patient and don't give up. Make sure you work hard and do everything you can to make your dreams come true.

Work on your image

As a reality star, the image you portray to the public is crucial. It can determine how successful you are in the industry and how the audience responds to you. In this sense, it is important to work on your image to constantly improve and refine it. Here are some tips on how to work on your image as a reality star. One of the most important things you can do as a reality star is to be authentic. This means that you show your true self in every situation and don't have to pretend or pretend to look good in front of the camera. If you are authentic, the audience will feel it and it will be much easier to connect with the viewers. Positivity is a key element to succeeding as a reality star. This doesn't mean that you have to always be happy or not talk about difficult situations, but rather that you have an optimistic attitude and make the best of every situation. If you are positive, the audience will appreciate it and you will be seen as inspiring and motivating. As a reality star, it is important to look good and groom yourself well. This doesn't mean that you have to look perfect, but rather that you take care of your appearance and make sure that you are always presentable. One should dress well and ensure that the makeup and hairstyle are always perfect. As a reality star, you should be versatile and able to adapt to different situations and roles. You shouldn't commit to a certain style or topic, but rather be flexible and willing to try new things. The more versatile you are, the more attractive you become to the audience. In today's world, social media is an important part of one's image as a reality star. One should make sure to build a strong social media presence and post content regularly to keep the audience engaged. Care should also be taken to build a clear and consistent brand that works both on and off camera. Success as a reality star doesn't come overnight. It requires hard work, perseverance and commitment. You should be willing to work hard and always be looking for new opportunities. If you work hard, you will ultimately be successful and improve your image as a reality star. Being a reality star gives you a platform and a voice that can be used to do good. You should therefore get involved in charity work and charitable projects.

Always be prepared

Living as a reality star can be a very exciting experience, but it can also be very stressful. The world of reality television is all about being authentic and natural, but that doesn't mean you shouldn't be prepared. Below are some tips on how you can always be prepared to succeed as a reality star. As a reality star, it's all about your story. The better you know your story, the better you can present it. Take time to reflect on your story and look at your past to find what makes you unique. You should be able to summarize your story in a few short sentences and be ready to tell it in any situation. Be aware that everything is being recorded. As a reality star, it is important to be aware that everything is being recorded. Every gesture, every sound and every reaction will be recorded and available for the world to see. Be aware of this and be conscious of what you do and what you say. It can be helpful to make a mental note of everything you say or do to ensure you always present yourself in your best light. Be prepared to express your opinion. As a reality star, you are expected to express your opinion on various topics and situations. It is important that you prepare and think through your opinion in advance. Think about how you feel about certain topics and questions and how you can communicate your thoughts in a clear and concise way. You need to be open and flexible. There are many unforeseen events and situations that can arise and it is important that you are prepared to adapt. Be willing to open yourself up to new experiences and interact with new people. Show your personality and be ready to step out of your comfort zone. Although life as a reality star may seem exciting and glamorous, it's also a business. As a reality star, you must be willing to work hard and negotiate hard to get the most out of your career. Be aware that the decisions you make can affect not only your personal life but also your career. 6. Work hard on your image As a reality star, it is important to work hard on your image. Be aware of how you present yourself and how you are perceived by others. Take time to plan your wardrobe and ensure you always appear in your best light. Be prepared to work hard to advance your career by showcasing yourself on social media platforms.

Work on your body

As a reality star, your body is often an important part of your image and career. Working on your body to stay fit and healthy will not only make you look better, but also make you feel better and help your career. Here are some tips on how to work on your body as a reality star. Find a workout routine that suits you. There are many ways to exercise your body. If you're a reality star, you probably have a busy schedule. That's why you should find a workout routine that fits your schedule. Maybe you only have half an hour a day to exercise. In this case, you could try a HIT (High Intensity Interval Training) routine, where you perform short but intense exercises that get your cardiovascular system going and burn calories. If you have more time, you could opt for yoga or Pilates to improve your flexibility and muscle strength. A healthy diet is an important factor in keeping your body in shape. As a reality star, you probably have a lot of commitments and may be tempted to eat fast and unhealthy foods. Try to keep healthy snacks like nuts, fruits, and vegetables within reach to avoid cravings. Make sure you eat enough protein to support your muscles, but limit your carbohydrate and sugar consumption. If you're having trouble achieving a balanced diet, you can work with a nutritionist to create a plan tailored to your needs. Adequate fluid intake is important to keep your body in shape. Drink enough water to hydrate your body and flush out toxins. If you have trouble drinking enough water, you can make infusions of fruits and vegetables to make the water tastier. It can be difficult to motivate yourself on your own. Find a workout partner to work out together or join a gym to do motivating group workouts with others. You can also hire a personal trainer to create a customized training program tailored to your needs. Keep a journal to track your progress in training and nutrition. This will help you stay motivated and achieve your goals. You can also take photos of yourself to see your progress and remind yourself how far you've come. As a reality star, it can be tempting to resort to extreme diets or training methods

Change your appearance

As a reality star, looks are an important factor that attracts a lot of consideration and attention. There are various ways to change the appearance and improve your own look. This article will introduce some of the most effective ways to create a new look as a reality star. One of the easiest and fastest ways to change your appearance is to change your hairstyle. A new hairstyle can emphasize the face in a completely new way and completely change the look. As a reality star, it is important to choose a hairstyle that stands out and attracts attention. This can include extravagant colors, eye-catching cuts or unusual styling. Can also play a big role in changing and improving the appearance. With skillful use of make-up, certain facial features can be highlighted or concealed. The same applies here: as a reality star, your make-up can be eye-catching and extravagant. Especially at public appearances and events, the make-up can be a little more in order to attract even more attention. New clothes can also completely change your appearance. Especially as a reality star, it is important to always keep up with the latest fashion and trends. Eye-catching colors, patterns and unusual cuts are not uncommon. Of course, clothing should always correspond to your own style and underline your character. In order to cut a good figure as a reality star, it is important to pay attention to physical fitness. Regular exercise and a healthy diet help tone the body and keep it fit. Through training, certain areas of the body can be specifically trained and thus improved. As a reality star, you should always make sure to cut a good figure and present yourself in top shape. Cosmetic surgery is also an option to change your appearance. However, it should always be remembered that this is a serious procedure and can involve risks. Even as a reality star, you should think carefully about whether cosmetic surgery is really necessary and what risks are associated with it. Piercings and tattoos are another way to change and individualize your appearance. However, you should make sure that the piercings and tattoos fit your own style and are not too exaggerated. As a reality star, you can also be a little bolder and, for example, wear noticeable facial piercings or large tattoos. In conclusion, there are many ways to change your appearance as a reality star. However, it is important that you remain true to yourself and emphasize your own style.

Create a lifestyle

Being a reality star is all about showcasing your personality and life in a way that grabs people's attention and makes them connect with you. It's about building a brand and creating an image that will be admired by your fans and followers. Here are some steps you can take to create a successful reality star lifestyle. There are many types of reality stars - from those focused on food and cooking, to fashion and beauty, to sports and fitness. Find what you do best and what you enjoy the most and focus on that. If you want to create a reality star lifestyle, you have to be authentic. Show your personality and be honest and open. Your fans will appreciate it when they feel like they really know you. Social media is an important part of a reality star's life. Use platforms like Instagram, TikTok, YouTube or Facebook to share your life and keep your fans up to date. Show what you eat, what you wear, where you are and who you spend time with. It's not just about having a following - it's about building a community. Respond to comments and messages, involve your fans in your decisions, and encourage them to connect with each other. One way to monetize your lifestyle as a reality star is to collaborate with brands. Find brands that match your image and niche and work with them to create sponsored content. To be successful you have to be creative. Find new ways to showcase your personality and lifestyle. Be experimental and try things that will set you apart from other reality stars. If you want to create a reality star lifestyle, you need to build a brand. Develop a logo and color scheme that fits your image and use it across all your platforms. Also consider merchandising to market your brand. It can be difficult to succeed as a reality star. It requires hard work and perseverance. Be prepared to face setbacks and don't give up when things get difficult. As a reality star you always have to be present. It's about staying in the conversation and constantly offering your fans new content. It can be helpful to create a content calendar to ensure you always have enough content. 10. Be grateful: Finally, it is important

Expand your business

As a reality star, you have the opportunity to expand your business in a variety of ways. Here are some tips on how you can achieve this. You probably have a large number of followers on social media platforms like Instagram, Twitter, and Facebook. Use this exposure to promote your business by posting regularly about your products or services. You could also organize live streams or Q&A sessions to answer questions from your fans and promote your business. If you're a reality star, you probably have a strong personality and a loyal fan base. Use this to create your own products tailored to your style and interests. For example, you could launch your own clothing line, jewelry collection, or fragrance line. As a reality star, you may already be a brand ambassador for various products. Use this experience to partner with brands that fit your business. For example, if you're a fitness guru, you could collaborate with a sportswear brand or design your own line of sports equipment. If you have a skill or knowledge that might be interesting to your fans, create online courses or tutorials. This can range from makeup tutorials to cooking classes to fitness workouts. These courses can be paid and can provide you with an additional source of income. Another way to expand your business as a reality star is to sell merchandise. Create t-shirts, hoodies, mugs or other products with your name, logo or sayings that your fans like. You could sell these products through your social media channels or create your own online store. If you enjoy organizing parties or attending events, use this skill to become an event organizer. For example, you could organize your own club night or music festival. Again, you could sell merchandise or your own products to expand your business. You want to expand your business as a reality star, you should expand your audience. Take the opportunity to participate in other reality shows or TV productions to grow your audience and increase your exposure. Attending events or conferences can also help you gain new fans and potential customers. If you enjoy speaking or chatting with other reality stars or industry experts.

Expand your knowledge

As a reality star, life revolves around the public and your own brand. To be successful, reality stars must constantly expand and improve their knowledge and skills. Here are some ways reality stars can expand their knowledge. Whether it's cooking, dancing, or acting, reality stars need to constantly learn new skills and improve their existing skills. By taking time to learn new skills, they can improve their career and their brand. Reading books is a great way to gain knowledge and insight. Reality stars can read books that focus on their careers, but also books about topics that interest them. Reading books can also help boost their creativity and improve their mental health. There are many classes that reality stars can take to improve their skills. Courses can take place online or in person and range from acting courses to business courses. By taking courses, reality stars can expand their knowledge and learn valuable new skills. A strong network can be invaluable for reality stars. By connecting with other people in their industry, they can gain inspiration, learn from others, and create new business opportunities. It is important that reality stars strive to build a network based on mutual benefit and support. By traveling and experiencing new cultures, reality stars can expand their understanding of the world and enhance their creativity. Traveling can also help them find new ideas for projects and content, helping them expand their brand. Social media is an important platform for reality stars to showcase their brand and connect with fans. By using social media, they can also learn from other people in their industry and receive valuable feedback. However, it is important that reality stars use social media wisely and strive to build an authentic and positive presence. Charity projects can help reality stars increase their exposure and have a positive impact on the world. By supporting a good cause, reality stars can also gain valuable experience and new perspectives. Overall, there are many ways reality stars can expand their knowledge.

Learn from other reality stars

Reality stars are personalities who have achieved a certain level of fame by making their lives public on television or social media platforms. Many of them have also learned a lesson or two that they can share with others. Here are some of them. In the world of reality television, it's important to establish yourself as a brand. Most successful reality stars have a strong presence on social media platforms and use it to promote their brand and generate new business opportunities. This means that they always pay attention to how they can influence their brand in their behavior and decisions. An example of this is the Kardashian-Jenner family. Many reality stars have learned that it's important to listen to their gut. In the world of reality television there are many unpredictable situations and sometimes you have to make decisions quickly. If you trust your instincts in these situations, you can often make better decisions. An example of this is former Bachelorette and Bachelor contestant Rachel Lindsay, who has often emphasized the importance of listening to your intuition. Successful reality stars often have a clear vision for their careers and lives. They know exactly what they want to achieve and work hard to achieve their goals. An example of this is former America's Next Top Model contestant and current entrepreneur Tyra Banks, who has always had a clear vision for her career and worked hard to achieve her goals. In the world of reality television, there are many opportunities to make mistakes. However, successful reality stars have learned that it's important to learn from these mistakes and improve. An example of this is former Real Housewives of Beverly Hills star Lisa Vanderpump, who has publicly admitted that she has learned from mistakes and strives to avoid them in the future. Stay authentic. In the world of reality television, there is often a pressure to play a certain role or display a certain personality. However, successful reality stars have learned that it's important to remain authentic and true to themselves. An example of this is former Real Housewives of New York City star Bethenny Frankel, who has often emphasized the importance of being yourself and not trying to be someone else. 6. Have a Strong Support System Successful reality stars often have a strong support system that helps them achieve their goals.

Stay up to date

Reality stars are people who have gained fame through their participation in reality shows. They have millions of fans around the world and are considered idols by many. Although they are admired by many, life as a reality star is not always easy. One of the most important things reality stars need to do to stay successful is stay relevant. You need to always keep up with the conversation and keep up to date with what's going on in the world. To do this, they need to be active on social media and regularly post new content that interests their fans. They should also attend public events and other events to maintain their public presence. Reality stars should consider their personality and image as a brand. They should work hard to shape their image and ensure that it is consistent with their values and beliefs. They should also work to monetize their brand by selling products associated with their image and personality. While it's important to stay relevant as a reality star, it's also important to stay true to yourself. Reality stars shouldn't change too much or give up their personality to become more popular. Instead, they should focus on what makes them unique and their fans will love them for it. Reality stars should always be open to new opportunities and be willing to step out of their comfort zone. They should be willing to try out new shows, movies, or other projects to advance their career. You should also be willing to collaborate with other reality stars and celebrities to increase their public presence. Although it looks easy to be successful as a reality star, it is actually hard work. Reality stars have to work hard to advance their careers and stay relevant. They must be willing to work long hours and perform even when tired or exhausted. They should also work hard to perfect their craft and improve their skills as entertainers. Reality stars should also maintain their relationships with other reality stars and celebrities. They should build friendships with other reality stars to advance their careers and discover new opportunities. They should also maintain good relationships with journalists and other media personalities to increase their media exposure. Although reality stars have many fans and are admired by many, they should remain down to earth. You shouldn't get too excited about your success

Fulfill your responsibilities as a reality star

As a reality star, you are in a unique position to influence people and society as a whole. It is important that you take your responsibilities as a public figure seriously and be aware that your actions can have repercussions. Here are some things you can do to fulfill your responsibilities as a reality star. As a reality star, you have many fans and followers. People look up to you and take their cue from you. Therefore, it is important that you are a positive role model. Behave respectfully, kindly and responsibly. Show that you are a good person who cares about others. It can be tempting to seek attention through scandals. But remember that your behavior can have consequences. Getting caught up in scandals can damage your career and image. Therefore, avoid risky or inappropriate behavior and act carefully. As a reality star, you have a voice and reach. Use this to draw attention to important social issues and bring about positive change. Donate money or your time to charities, support campaigns and show your commitment. Be honest and authentic in your behavior and personality. Don't pretend or try to be someone other than who you really are. People value genuineness and authenticity and will respect you for it. Be aware that your actions can have repercussions. As a public figure, you have a greater responsibility than the average person. Your actions can have repercussions and influence people. Be aware of this and act accordingly. Remember that your words and actions will be noticed by many people and that you can have a positive or negative influence. Respect other people regardless of their background, gender or age. Avoid insulting or discriminating against others. Show that you are a tolerant and respectful person.

As a public person, you should obey laws and rules. Do not behave inappropriately or unethically and abide by applicable rules and regulations. Overall, it's important that you take your responsibilities as a reality star seriously. You have the opportunity to have a positive impact on people and society. Use this opportunity to serve as a good role model and advocate for positive change. Be authentic, respectful and responsible and avoid inappropriate behavior or scandals.

Conclusion reality

Star As a reality star, I can say that being in the spotlight is a very exciting and unique experience. The ability to have fans and be recognized by people on the street is very satisfying and makes it easy to feel important and valued. However, there are also many challenges and difficulties that come with being a reality star. On the one hand, you have to constantly be on your guard because you are constantly in the public eye. Every action, every word and every gesture can be picked up and analyzed by fans and the media. This can be very stressful and stressful as you constantly have to be aware that you are being watched. Another problem is privacy. As a reality star, you have to be aware that you no longer have the same kind of privacy as other people. The fans and media want to know everything you do, and you can't just retreat into a quiet life without it being noticed. This can be very limiting and stressful, especially if you don't feel like you can fully open up. You also have to be aware that life as a reality star cannot last. Most reality shows have a limited run, and once the show is over, it can be difficult to retain the attention and fans you gained during the show. One must be aware that a career as a reality star can be very short-lived and one must prepare for other opportunities to stay in the spotlight. Despite these challenges, I can say that I have thoroughly enjoyed life as a reality star. It has given me the opportunity to meet new people, travel to new places and do things I would never have done otherwise. It also gave me the opportunity to show my personality and skills and develop as a person. Overall, I think life as a reality star is an experience that can be enjoyed as long as you understand that there will be challenges and difficulties. You have to be aware that you are in the public eye and that your every move is being watched. You also have to be prepared to prepare for other career opportunities if your time as a reality star is over. All in all, I think life as a reality star is an exciting and unique experience worth having if you accept the challenges and difficulties and are willing to adapt and grow. I am grateful for the opportunity to be a reality star and I think I have learned a lot and grown as a person through this experience.

imprint / copyright 2023

Luna Ludwig
Am Anger 3
06869 Coswig
Germany
Luna-Publishing.de